Film stars ▪ *Stars* ▪ Filmstars

Photographs of Magnum Photos • *Photographies de Magnum Photos* • **Fotografien von Magnum Photos**

·TERRAIL·
PHOTO

■ Editor: Jean-Claude Dubost
Desk Editor: Caroline Broué
Graphic design: Véronique Rossi
Iconographic and artistic coordination at Magnum Photos:
Marie-Christine Biebuyck and Agnès Sire,
assisted by Philippe Devernay, Marta Campos and Inessa Quenum
English translation: Glenn Naumovitz
Photoengraving: Litho Service T. Zamboni, Verona

© FINEST SA / EDITIONS PIERRE TERRAIL, Paris, 1998
The Art Book Subsidiary of BAYARD PRESSE SA
Magnum Photos, Paris, 1998
ISBN 2-87939-197-0
English edition: © 1998
Publication number: 240
Printed in Italy.

■ *Direction éditoriale : Jean-Claude Dubost*
Assistante éditoriale : Caroline Broué
Conception et réalisation graphique : Véronique Rossi
Direction iconographique et artistique à Magnum Photos :
Marie-Christine Biebuyck et Agnès Sire,
assistées de Philippe Devernay, Marta Campos et Inessa Quenum
Traduction anglaise : Glenn Naumovitz
Traduction allemande : Inge Hanneforth
Photogravure : Litho Service T. Zamboni, Vérone

© FINEST SA / ÉDITIONS PIERRE TERRAIL, Paris, 1998
La filiale Livres d'art de BAYARD PRESSE SA
Magnum Photos, Paris, 1998
ISBN 2-87939-188-1
N° d'éditeur : 240
Dépôt légal : octobre 1998
Imprimé en Italie.

■ Verlegerische Leitung: Jean-Claude Dubost
Verantwortlich für die Ausgabe: Caroline Broué
Buchgestaltung: Véronique Rossi
Bildredaktion und gragische Gestaltung für Magnum Photos:
Marie-Christine Biebuyck, Agnès Sire;
Assistenten: Philippe Devernay, Marta Campos, Inessa Quenum
Deutsche Übersetzung: Inge Hanneforth
Farblithos: Litho Service T. Zamboni, Verona

© FINEST SA / EDITIONS PIERRE TERRAIL, Paris, 1998
Der Bereich Kunstbücher von BAYARD PRESSE SA
Magnum Photos, Paris, 1998
ISBN 2-87939-197-0
Deutsche Ausgabe: © 1998
Verlegernummer: 240
Printed in Italy.

Gong Li glowing in the spotlights, Paul Newman concentrating during a class at the Actor's Studio, Gary Cooper going fishing, Nanni Moretti on his scooter, Ingrid Bergman on the set of a Hitchcock film and Simone Signoret and Yves Montand after the Oscar awards ceremony are some of the stars who were caught by surprise or agreed to pose for the photographers whose pictures appear in this book. The situations are highly diversified, creating a rich and varied collection.

The diversity of the figures and situations captured on film is further enhanced by the plurality of looks in each one of these portraits. From faces that wonderfully capture light, illuminated by the halo of a spotlight, to casual, natural actors in 'real life', the very image of the star changes. Whether they are legendary because of their beauty, like the Hollywood stars of the fifties who strike majestic poses, or because of their faces, their presence and their individuality, the pictures of movie stars we have decided to present in this book demonstrate a wide variety of personalities and looks. Unexpected images are side by side, such as Elizabeth Taylor and Marilyn Monroe posing as glamour girls for Philippe Halsman, and more unusual pictures that break with the frozen image actors often give of themselves, such as Woody Allen playing the clarinet in a jazz club or Juliette Binoche in an extreme close-up. Stars can also play frivolous roles, dancing or laughing between takes. That lightness contrasts with the concentration of the actor at work, alone or with the director, which is another strong image of the star, this time in the middle of making a film. Lastly, the actor's second face, one that could seem ambiguous, is hidden behind Toshiro Mifune in the semi-darkness of a smoke-filled room, Marlene Dietrich seen from behind at Columbia studios, Anna Magnani with a tormented look on her face and Charlie Chaplin in front of his mirror. Face to face with themselves, are they dreaming, doubting or concentrating? Mysterious, weary or anxious?

The diversity of gestures, situations and looks is what makes a topic like this one so rich. The images of stars in every situation and every mood offered in this book break with the familiar clichés, without shattering the magic of a world peopled by dreams and legends.

Jean-Claude Dubost

Gong Li rayonnant dans la lumière des projecteurs, Paul Newman concentré pendant un cours à l'Actor's Studio, Gary Cooper allant à la pêche, Nanni Moretti sur son scooter, Ingrid Bergman lors du tournage d'un film d'Hitchcock, Simone Signoret et Yves Montand après la cérémonie des Oscars... Ces stars se sont laissé surprendre ou ont accepté de poser pour les photographes dans des situations d'une extrême diversité, créant un ensemble riche et varié.

La diversité des figures et des situations saisies s'enrichit en outre de la pluralité des regards qui s'appliquent à chacun de ces portraits. Des visages qui captent merveilleusement la lumière, éclairés par le halo d'un projecteur, à l'acteur hors de sa situation professionnelle, léger, naturel, c'est l'image même de la star qui change. Qu'elles soient mythiques pour leur beauté, tels les acteurs hollywoodiens des années 50 qui posent avec majesté, ou pour leur « gueule », leur présence, les stars que nous avons choisi de montrer témoignent ici des variations de leur personnalité et de leur représentation.

Dès lors, se mêlent images attendues, telle Elizabeth Taylor ou Marylin Monroe posant en glamour pour Philippe Halsman, et photos plus insolites qui rompent avec l'image figée que l'acteur donne souvent de lui-même, tel Woody Allen faisant de la musique dans une boîte de jazz, ou Juliette Binoche en très gros plan. Les stars peuvent aussi jouer les frivoles, danser ou rire entre deux prises... Cette légèreté contraste avec la concentration de l'acteur au travail, seul ou en compagnie du réalisateur qui le dirige, ce qui est encore une autre image forte de la star, cette fois-ci en plein tournage.

Enfin, derrière Toshiro Mifune dans la semi-obscurité d'une pièce enfumée, Marlene Dietrich, de dos, attendant l'heure d'enregistrement aux studios Columbia, Anna Magnani, l'air tourmenté, ou encore Charlie Chaplin devant son miroir, se cache un dernier visage de l'acteur qui peut paraître ambigu : face à lui-même, songeur, dubitatif, concentré, mystérieux, las, anxieux... ? Cette diversité des gestes, des situations et des regards crée la richesse d'un sujet comme celui-ci. C'est bien une image de la star « dans tous ses états » que nous proposons, qui rompt avec les clichés sans briser la magie d'un univers peuplé de rêves et de mythes.

Jean-Claude Dubost

Die unter den Lichtern der Projektoren strahlende Gong Li, der beim Schauspielunterricht im Actor's Studio konzentrierte Paul Newman, Gary Cooper, der angeln geht, Nanni Moretti auf seinem Motorroller, Ingrid Bergman beim Drehen eines Hitchcock-Films, Simone Signoret und Yves Montand nach der Oscar-Verleihung ... All diese Stars ließen sich in den unterschiedlichsten Situationen überraschen oder akzeptierten es, für die Fotografen zu posieren.

Die vielfältigen Gesichter und eingefangenen Momente erlauben die unterschiedlichsten Betrachtungsweisen eines jeden Porträts. Angefangen von Gesichtern, die auf wunderbare Art vom Licht der Projektoren beleuchtet sind bis hin zum unbesorgt und natürlich wirkenden Schauspieler außerhalb seines professionellen Umfelds entdeckt man den Star einmal ganz anders. Mag er, wie in den fünfziger Jahren, mythisch sein aufgrund seiner Schönheit oder seines markanten Gesichts - die Präsenz, die Persönlichkeit der Stars, die wir ausgewählt haben, bezeugen ihre Vielschichtigkeit in jeder Hinsicht.

Hier vermischen sich mehr oder weniger erwartete Aufnahmen von Elizabeth Taylor oder Marylin Monroe, die für Philippe Halsman eine Glamour-Pose einnehmen, mit ungewöhnlichen Fotos, die mit dem rigiden Bild brechen, das der Schauspieler oft von sich selbst gibt, so etwa Woody Allen, der in einem Jazzclub spielt, oder Juliette Binoche in einem besonders nahen Close-up. Auch sieht man Stars in frivoler Pose, solche die tanzen oder in den Drehpausen entspannt lachen ... Diese Leichtigkeit kontrastiert mit der Konzentration des Schauspielers bei der Arbeit, allein oder mit dem Regisseur, der ihm Anweisungen gibt, was ein ganz anderes, eindrucksvolles Bild des Stars zeigt. Und schließlich, hinter Toshiro Mifune im Halbdunkel eines verrauchten Raumes, Marlene Dietrich von hinten, auf ihre Gesangsaufnahmen in den Columbia Studios wartend, Anna Magnani mit verstörtem Gesicht oder aber Charlie Chaplin vor seinem Spiegel. Hier verbirgt sich ein ganz anderes Gesicht des Schauspielers: sich selbst gegenübergestellt, nachdenklich, zweifelnd, konzentriert, mysteriös, müde, ängstlich ...

All diese unterschiedlichen Haltungen, Umstände und Blicke schaffen die Vielfältigkeit eines solchen Themas. Was wir hier zeigen, ist das Bild des Stars in den unterschiedlichsten Augenblicken. Das bricht zwar mit den Klischees, bewahrt aber die Magie eines Universums voller Träume und Mythen.

Jean-Claude Dubost

Orson Welles. Nicolas Tikhomiroff, Spain, *Espagne,* Spanien, 1964. | **7**

8 | **Sophia Loren.** Elliott Erwitt, France, *France,* Frankreich, 1962.

Marylin Monroe. Elliott Erwitt, USA, *États-Unis,* USA, 1960.

10 Gérard Philipe & Jeanne Valérie. Burt Glinn, France, *France,* Frankreich, 1959.

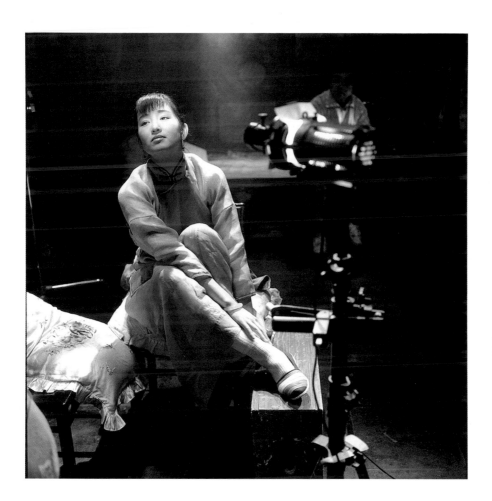

Gong Li. Patrick Zachmann, China, *Chine,* China, 1995. **11**

Jean-Luc Godard. Gilles Peress, France, *France,* Frankreich, 1985. **13**

Woody Allen. Gilles Peress, USA, *États-Unis,* USA, 1980. **15**

16 | Gary Cooper. Robert Capa, USA, *États-Unis,* USA, 1941.

Isabella Rossellini. Eve Arnold, USA, *États-Unis,* USA, 1995. | **17**

18 | Brigitte Bardot. Burt Glinn, France, *France,* Frankreich, 1958.

Isabelle Huppert. Josef Koudelka, France, *France,* Frankreich, 1985. | **19**

Katherine Hepburn. Bob Henriques, USA, *États-Unis,* USA, 1961.

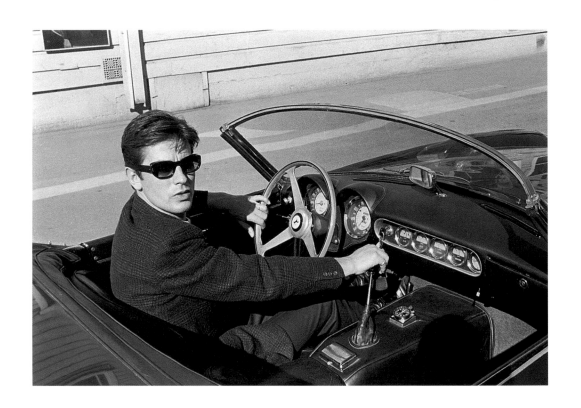

Nanni Moretti. Harry Gruyaert, Italy, *Italie,* Italien, 1994.

Clark Gable. Eve Arnold, USA, *États-Unis,* USA, 1960.

26 | **Faye Dunaway & Marcello Mastroianni.** Nicolas Tikhomiroff. Italy, *Italie,* Italien, 1968.

Monica Vitti & Terence Stamp. Eve Arnold, England, *Angleterre,* England, 1965. | **27**

28 John Huston & Colette Marchand. Robert Capa, France, *France,* Frankreich, 1952.

Ava Gardner. Robert Capa, Spain, *Espagne,* Spanien, 1954. |**29**

John Wayne. Dennis Stock, USA, *États-Unis,* USA, 1959.

32 | François Truffaut & Oskar Werner. Philippe Halsman, France, *France,* Frankreich, 1966.

Alfred Hitchcock & Ingrid Bergman. Robert Capa, USA, *États-Unis,* USA, 1946. **33**

| Claudia Cardinale. George Rodger, Spain, *Espagne,* Spanien, 1965.

Richard Avedon & Fred Astaire. David Seymour, USA, *États-Unis,* USA, 1956. **35**

Marylin Monroe. Eve Arnold, USA, *États-Unis,* USA, 1960.

38 | **Humphrey Bogart.** Philippe Halsman, USA, *États-Unis,* USA, 1944.

Grace Kelly. Philippe Halsman, USA, *États-Unis,* USA, 1954. | **39**

Dustin Hoffman & Mia Farrow. Philippe Halsman, USA, *États-Unis,* USA, 1969.

Elizabeth Taylor. Philippe Halsman, USA, *États-Unis,* USA, 1948. **41**

| Vivien Leigh & Laurence Olivier. Philippe Halsman, USA, *États-Unis,* USA, 1951.

Lauren Bacall. Philippe Halsman, USA, *États-Unis,* USA, 1944.

44 | **Sean Connery.** George Rodger, England, *Angleterre,* England, 1964.

Rita Hayworth. Philippe Halsman, USA, *États-Unis,* USA, 1950. **45**

46 | **Tippi Hedren.** Philippe Halsman, USA, *États-Unis,* USA, 1962.

Gloria Swanson. Philippe Halsman, USA, *États-Unis,* USA, 1950. **47**

Juliette Binoche. Gilles Peress, France, *France,* Frankreich, 1985\ **49**

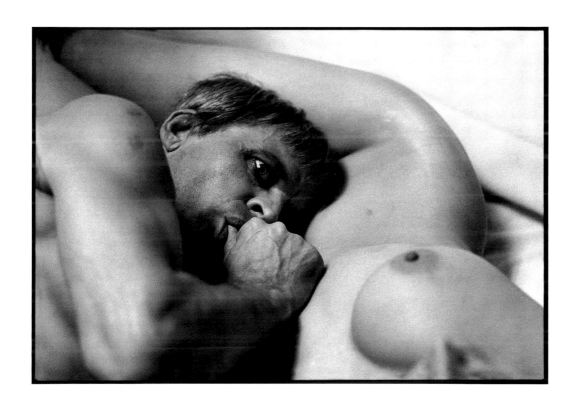

Klaus Kinski. Jean Gaumy, France, *France,* Frankreich, 1974.

| Marlene Dietrich. Eve Arnold, USA, *États-Unis,* USA, 1952.

James Dean. Dennis Stock, USA, *États-Unis,* USA, 1955. **53**

54 | Toshiro Mifune. Werner Bischof, Japan, *Japon,* Japan, 1951.

Harvey Keitel & Gian Maria Volonte. Josef Koudelka, Bosnia-Herzegovina, *Bosnie-Herzégovine,* Bosnien-Herzegowina, 1994. 55

| Charlie Chaplin. W. Eugene Smith, USA, *États-Unis,* USA, 1952.

Anna Magnani. Philippe Halsman, Italy, *Italie,* Italien, 1951.

Simone Signoret & Yves Montand. Dennis Stock, USA, *États-Unis,* USA, 1960.

Page 7: Orson Welles during the making of *Chimes at Midnight* in Spain. Nicolas Tikhomiroff, 1964.
Page 7 : *Orson Welles pendant le tournage du film* Falstaff *en Espagne. Nicolas Tikhomiroff, 1964.*
Seite 7: Orson Welles bei den Dreharbeiten des Films *Falstaff* in Spanien. Nicolas Tikhomiroff, 1964.

Page 8: Sophia Loren during the making of *Five Miles to Midnight*, directed by Anatole Litvak. Paris, France. Elliott Erwitt, 1962.
Page 8 : *Sophia Loren pendant le tournage du film* Le Couteau dans la plaie, *d'Anatole Litvak. Paris, France. Elliott Erwitt, 1962.*
Seite 8: Sophia Loren bei den Dreharbeiten von *Le Couteau dans la plaie* von Anatole Litvak. Paris, Frankreich. Elliott Erwitt, 1962.

Page 9: Marylin Monroe watching the rushes of the film she is making, *The Misfits*, by John Huston. California, USA. Elliott Erwitt, 1960.
Page 9 : *Marylin Monroe regardant les rushes du film* Les Désaxés *de John Huston. Californie, États-Unis. Elliott Erwitt, 1960.*
Seite 9: Marylin Monroe bei der Ansicht der Rushes des Films *Nicht gesellschaftsfähig* von John Huston. Kalifornien, USA. Elliott Erwitt, 1960.

Page 10: Gérard Philipe et Jeanne Valérie during the making of *Les Liaisons dangereuses*, directed by Roger Vadim. France. Burt Glinn, 1959.
Page 10 : *Gérard Philipe et Jeanne Valérie pendant le tournage du film* Les Liaisons dangereuses, *réalisé par Roger Vadim. France. Burt Glinn, 1959.*
Seite 10: Gérard Philipe und Jeanne Valérie bei den Dreharbeiten des Films *Gefährliche Liebschaften* von Roger Vadim. Frankreich. Burt Glinn, 1959.

Page 11: The actress Gong Li during the making of the film *Temptress Moon*, directed by Chen Kaige. China. Patrick Zachmann, 1995.
Page 11 : *L'actrice Gong Li sur le tournage du film* Temptress Moon, *réalisé par Chen Kaige. Chine. Patrick Zachmann, 1995.*
Seite 11: Die Schauspielerin Gong Li bei den Dreharbeiten von *Temptress Moon* von Chen Kaige. China. Patrick Zachmann, 1995.

Pages 12-13: Jean-Luc Godard adjusts the focus of his film *Detective* for the Cannes International Film Festival. France, Gilles Peress, 1985.
Pages 12-13 : *Jean-Luc Godard règle la projection de son film* Détective, *pour le Festival international du cinéma à Cannes. France, Gilles Peress, 1985.*
Seite 12-13: Jean-Luc Godard bei der Einstellung des Projektors vor der Vorführung seines Films *Detektiv* während des Filmfestivals von Cannes. Frankreich, Gilles Peress, 1985.

Page 15: Woody Allen and his jazz band at Michael's Pub. Manhattan, New York City, USA. Gilles Peress, 1980.
Page 15 : *Woody Allen et son orchestre de jazz au Michael's Pub. Manhattan, New York, États-Unis. Gilles Peress, 1980.*
Seite 15: Woody Allen und seine Jazzband im Michael's Pub. Manhattan, New York, USA. Gilles Peress, 1980.

Page 16: Gary Cooper going fishing in Sun Valley, Idaho, USA. Robert Capa, 1941.
Page 16 : *Gary Cooper allant à la pêche à Sun Valley, Idaho, États-Unis. Robert Capa, 1941.*
Seite 16: Gary Cooper geht angeln in Sun Valley, Idaho, USA. Robert Capa, 1941.

Page 17: Isabella Rossellini modelling Betsy Johnson (on the left) clothes. New York, USA. Eve Arnold, 1995.
Page 17 : *Isabella Rossellini essayant les vêtements de Betsy Johnson (à gauche). New York, États-Unis. Eve Arnold, 1995.*
Seite 17: Isabella Rossellini bei der Anprobe der Kleidung von Betsy Johnson (links). New York, USA. Eve Arnold, 1995.

Page 18: Brigitte Bardot in Saint-Tropez (and playing the guitar the singer Sacha Distel), France. Burt Glinn, 1958.
Page 18 : *Brigitte Bardot à Saint-Tropez (à la guitare le chanteur Sacha Distel), France. Burt Glinn, 1958.*
Seite 18: Brigitte Bardot in Saint-Tropez (mit dem Gitarre spielenden Sänger Sacha Distel), Frankreich. Burt Glinn, 1958.

Page 19: Isabelle Huppert, Paris, France. Josef Koudelka, 1985.
Page 19 : *Isabelle Huppert, Paris, France. Josef Koudelka, 1985.*
Seite 19: Isabelle Huppert, Paris, Frankreich. Josef Koudelka, 1985.

Page 20: Katherine Hepburn during the making of *A long Day's Journey into Night*, directed by Sidney Lumet. USA. Bob Henriques, 1961.
Page 20 : *Katherine Hepburn pendant le tournage de* A long Day's Journey into Night, *réalisé par Sidney Lumet. États-Unis. Bob Henriques, 1961.*
Seite 20: Katherine Hepburn bei den Dreharbeiten von *A long Day's Journey into Night* von Sidney Lumet. USA. Bob Henriques, 1961.

Page 21: Paul Newman at the Actor's Studio. New York, USA. Eve Arnold, 1955.
Page 21 : *Paul Newman à l'Actor's Studio. New York, États-Unis. Eve Arnold, 1955.*
Seite 21: Paul Newman im

Actor's Studio, New York, USA.
Eve Arnold, 1955.

Page 22: Alain Delon during the making of *Once a Thief*, directed by Ralph Nelson. Hollywood, USA.
Wayne Miller, 1964.
Page 22 : *Alain Delon pendant le tournage du film* Les Tueurs de San Francisco, *réalisé par Ralph Nelson. Hollywood, États-Unis. Wayne Miller, 1964.*
Seite 22: Alain Delon bei den Dreharbeiten des Films *Once a Thief* von Ralph Nelson. Hollywood, USA. Wayne Miller, 1964.

Page 23: The Italian film director Nanni Moretti, director and actor of the film *Dear Diary*, in Rome, Italy.
Harry Gruyaert, 1994.
Page 23 : *Le cinéaste italien Nanni Moretti, réalisateur et acteur du film* Journal intime *à Rome, Italie. Harry Gruyaert, 1994.*
Seite 23: Der italienische Filmemacher Nanni Moretti ist Regisseur und Hauptdarsteller seines Films *Caro Diario*. Rom, Italien. Harry Gruyaert, 1994.

Page 25: Clark Gable during the making of *The Misfits*, directed by John Huston. Nevada, USA.
Eve Arnold, 1960.
Page 25 : *Clark Gable pendant le tournage du film* Les Désaxés, *de John Huston. Nevada, États-Unis. Eve Arnold, 1960.*
Seite 25: Clark Gable bei den Dreharbeiten des Films

Nicht gesellschaftsfähig von John Huston. Nevada, USA.
Eve Arnold, 1960.

Page 26: Marcello Mastroianni (as Valerio) and Faye Dunaway (as Julie) in *A Place for Lovers* (original title *Amanti*), directed by Vittorio De Sica. The scene is shot on location in the marshes between Venice and Ferrara, Italy.
Nicolas Tikhomiroff, 1968.
Page 26 : *Marcello Mastroianni (Valerio) et Faye Dunaway (Julie) dans* Le Temps des amants, *un film de Vittorio de Sica (titre original* Amanti*). La scène a été tournée dans les marais entre Venise et Ferrare, Italie. Nicolas Tikhomiroff, 1968.*
Seite 26: Marcello Mastroianni (Valerio) und Faye Dunaway (Julie) in *Amanti*, einem Film von Vittorio de Sica. Die Szene wurde im Marsch zwischen Venedig und Ferrara gedreht, Italien. Nicolas Tikhomiroff, 1968.

Page 27: Terence Stamp and Monica Vitti during the making of *Modesty Blaise*, directed by Joseph Losey. London, England.
Eve Arnold, 1965.
Page 27 : *Terence Stamp et Monica Vitti pendant le tournage de* Modesty Blaise, *réalisé par Joseph Losey. Londres, Angleterre. Eve Arnold, 1965.*
Seite 27: Terence Stamp und Monica Vitti bei den Dreharbeiten von *Modesty Blaise* von Joseph Losey.

London, England.
Eve Arnold, 1965.

Page 28: John Huston directing Colette Marchand in his film *Moulin Rouge*. Paris, France.
Robert Capa, 1952.
Page 28 : *John Huston dirigeant Colette Marchand pour son film* Moulin Rouge. *Paris, France. Robert Capa, 1952.*
Seite 28: John Huston gibt in seinem Film *Moulin Rouge* Colette Marchand Regieanweisungen. Paris, Frankreich. Robert Capa, 1952.

Page 29: Ava Gardner during the making of The *Barefoot Contessa*, directed by Joseph L. Mankiewicz, with Humphrey Bogart. Spain.
Robert Capa, 1954.
Page 29 : *Ava Gardner pendant le tournage du film* La Comtesse aux pieds nus, *réalisé par Joseph L. Mankiewicz, avec Humphrey Bogart. Espagne. Robert Capa, 1954.*
Seite 29: Ava Gardner bei den Dreharbeiten des Films *Die barfüßige Gräfin* (mit Humphrey Bogart) von Joseph L. Mankiewicz. Spanien. Robert Capa, 1954.

Pages 30-31: John Wayne during the making of the film *The Alamo*, directed and acted by John Wayne in 1959. USA.
Dennis Stock, 1959.
Pages 30-31 : *John Wayne lors du tournage de* Alamo, *qu'il réalisa et joua en 1959.*

États-Unis.
Dennis Stock, 1959.
Seite 30-31: John Wayne bei den Dreharbeiten des Films *Alamo* aus dem Jahr 1959, bei dem er Regie führt und in dem er die Hauptrolle spielt. USA. Dennis Stock, 1959.

Page 32: Oscar Werner and François Truffaut (on the right) during the making of *Fahrenheit 451*, directed by François Truffaut. Orléans, France.
Philippe Halsman, 1966.
Page 32 : *Oscar Werner et François Truffaut (à droite) lors du tournage de* Fahrenheit 451, *de François Truffaut. Orléans, France. Philippe Halsman, 1966.*
Seite 32: Oscar Werner und François Truffaut (rechts) bei den Dreharbeiten des Films *Fahrenheit 451* von François Truffaut. Orléans, Frankreich. Philippe Halsman, 1966.

Page 33: The director Alfred Hitchcock supervising the close-up frame of the cameraman directed on the hand of Ingrid Bergman during the filming of *Notorious*. Hollywood, USA.
Robert Capa, May 1946.
Page 33 : *Le réalisateur Alfred Hitchcock supervise le cadrage de la main de Ingrid Bergman pendant le tournage du film* Les Enchaînés. *Hollywood, États-Unis. Robert Capa, mai 1946.*
Seite 33: Alfred Hitchcock überwacht das Close-up von Ingrid Bergmans Hand bei den Dreharbeiten des Films

Weißes Gift (Notorious).
Hollywood, USA.
Robert Capa, Mai 1946.

■ **Page 34:** Claudia Cardinale during the making of *The Lost Command*, directed by Mark Robson. Near Almeria, Andalousia, Spain.
George Rodger, 1965.
Page 34 : *Claudia Cardinale lors du tournage du film Les Centurions, de Mark Robson. Près d'Almeria, Andalousie, Espagne.*
George Rodger, 1965.
Seite 34: Claudia Cardinale bei den Dreharbeiten des Films The Lost Command von Mark Robson in der Nähe von Almeria, Andalusien, Spanien.
George Rodger, 1965.

■ **Page 35:** Richard Avedon advises Fred Astaire on his role as a photographer in *Funny Face*. USA.
David Seymour, 1956.
Page 35 : *Richard Avedon conseille Fred Astaire dans le rôle d'un photographe dans Drôle de frimousse. États-Unis.*
David Seymour, 1956.
Seite 35: Richard Avedon berät Fred Astaire in der Rolle eines Fotografen im Film Funny Face. USA.
David Seymour, 1956.

■ **Page 37:** Marilyn Monroe resting between takes during a photographic studio session in Hollywood, for the making of *The Misfits*, directed by John Huston. USA.
Eve Arnold, 1960.
Page 37 : *Marilyn Monroe se reposant entre deux prises pendant une séance photo*

pour le tournage du film Les Désaxés, de John Huston. *États-Unis.*
Eve Arnold, 1960.
Seite 37: Marilyn Monroe, die sich zwischen zwei Aufnahmen in einem Fotostudio für die Dreharbeiten des Films Nicht gesellschaftsfähig von John Huston ausruht. USA.
Eve Arnold, 1960.

■ **Page 38:** Humphrey Bogart. USA. Philippe Halsman, 1944.
Page 38 : *Humphrey Bogart. États-Unis.*
Philippe Halsman, 1944.
Seite 38: Humphrey Bogart. USA. Philippe Halsman, 1944.

■ **Page 39:** Grace Kelly. New York, USA.
Philippe Halsman, 1954.
Page 39 : *Grace Kelly. New York, États-Unis.*
Philippe Halsman, 1954.
Seite 39: Grace Kelly. New York, USA.
Philippe Halsman, 1954.

■ **Page 40:** Mia Farrow and Dustin Hoffman during the filming of *John and Mary*, directed by Pater Yates. USA, Philippe Halsman, 1969.
Page 40 : *Mia Farrow et Dustin Hoffman pendant le tournage du film John et Mary, réalisé par Peter Yates. États-Unis.*
Philippe Halsman, 1969.
Seite 40: Mia Farrow und Dustin Hoffman bei den Dreharbeiten des Films John and Mary von Peter Yates. USA.
Philippe Halsman, 1969.

■ **Page 41:** Elizabeth Taylor.

New York, USA.
Philippe Halsman, 1948.
Page 41 : *Elizabeth Taylor. New York, États-Unis.*
Philippe Halsman, 1948.
Seite 41: Elizabeth Taylor. New York, USA.
Philippe Halsman, 1948.

■ **Page 42:** Vivien Leigh and Laurence Olivier. USA. Philippe Halsman, 1951.
Page 42 : *Vivien Leigh et Laurence Olivier. États-Unis.*
Philippe Halsman, 1951.
Seite 42: Vivien Leigh und Laurence Olivier. USA.
Philippe Halsman, 1951.

■ **Page 43:** Lauren Bacall. Hollywood, USA.
Philippe Halsman, 1944.
Page 43 : *Lauren Bacall. Hollywood, États-Unis.*
Philippe Halsman, 1944.
Seite 43: Lauren Bacall. Hollywood, USA.
Philippe Halsman, 1944.

■ **Page 44:** Sean Connery as James Bond during the filming of *Goldfinger*, directed by Guy Hamilton. London, England.
George Rodger, 1964.
Page 44 : *Sean Connery, dans le rôle de James Bond, lors du tournage du film Goldfinger, de Guy Hamilton. Londres, Angleterre.*
George Rodger, 1964.
Seite 44: Sean Connery, alias James Bond, bei den Dreharbeiten des Films Goldfinger, von Guy Hamilton. London, England.
George Rodger, 1964.

■ **Page 45:** Rita Hayworth posing in the studio of fashion

photographer George Hoyningen-Huene. USA.
Philippe Halsman, 1950.
Page 45 : *Rita Hayworth posant dans le studio du photographe de mode George Hoyningen-Huene. États-Unis.*
Philippe Halsman, 1950.
Seite 45: Rita Hayworth posiert im Studio des Modefotografen George Hoyningen-Huene. USA.
Philippe Halsman, 1950.

■ **Page 46:** Tippi Hedren, the actress of Alfred Hitchcock's film *The Birds*. USA.
Philippe Halsman, 1962.
Page 46 : *Tippi Hedren, la vedette du film d'Alfred Hitchcock Les Oiseaux. États-Unis.*
Philippe Halsman, 1962.
Seite 46: Tippi Hedren in der Hauprolle des Films von Alfred Hitchcock Die Vögel. USA.
Philippe Halsman, 1962.

■ **Page 47:** Portrait of Gloria Swanson, extract from the 101 covers that Philippe Halsman shot for *Life* magazine. USA.
Philippe Halsman, 1950.
Page 47 : *Portrait de Gloria Swanson, extrait des cent et une couvertures que Philippe Halsman a réalisées pour le magazine Life. États-Unis.*
Philippe Halsman, 1950.
Seite 47: Porträt von Gloria Swanson. Eines der hunderteins Titelfotos von Philippe Halsman für Life Magazine. USA.
Philippe Halsman, 1950.

■ **Page 49:** The French actress Juliette Binoche during the Cannes International Film